Rachel Crow:

From the Heart

by Riley Brooks

SCHOLASTIC INC.

Photographs © 2013

AP Images: cover (Dowling/PictureGroup); 7 (Donald Traill); 25 (Doug Sonders/iHeartRadio); 10 & 21 (Frank Micelotta/Fox/PictureGroup); 13 & 26 (Ray Mickshaw/Fox/PictureGroup); 14 (Leon/PictureGroup); 22 (Rex Features)

Corbis Images/Splash News: 1

Getty Images: back cover (Jordan Strauss/Invision); 4 (Eric Charbonneau); 5 & 9 (FOX), 17 (Neilson Barnard/ Nickelodeon); 18 (Rachel Murray); 29 (Frazer Harrison); 30 (Jeff Kravitz); 32 (Larry Busacca)

Shutterstock, Inc.: Color splashes throughout interior and front and back covers

Splash News: 6

© 2013 by Scholastic

ISBN 978-0-545-55000-0

Published by Scholastic Inc.

SCHOLASTIC and associated logos are trademarks and/or registered trademarks of Scholastic Inc.

12 11 10 9 8 7 6 5 4 3 2 1   13 14 15 16 17/0

Printed in the U.S.A.   40

First printing, January 2013

Table of Contents

Introduction:

Can you imagine performing in front of millions of people on national television? Well, that's how adorable pop princess Rachel Crow rose to fame—as the youngest contestant on the talent show *The X Factor*. Since then, she's gone on to win the hearts of fans around the world with her bubbly personality, amazing acting skills, and incredible singing voice. But things haven't always been so sunny for Rachel. She overcame a lot to achieve her dreams, and she has inspired everyone she's met with her talent, heart, and determination.

Chapter 1: Little Star

When Barbara and Kelly Crow
volunteered to serve as a foster family
in their small hometown of Mead, Colorado,
they had no idea how much their lives would
change. In July of 1998, they met adorable
six-month-old baby Rachel. Rachel had been
placed in the care of social services because
her mom had been hurting her. Barbara

and Kelly immediately fell in love with Rachel and set out to adopt her. Kelly ran a construction business in nearby Boulder, and Barbara was a counselor at a hospital in town, so she knew just how to help this little girl heal and feel loved and safe. When Rachel was one and a half years old, the Crow family officially adopted her, and Rachel has never looked back. Some kids may have wanted to meet their birth

parents, but not Rachel. "I have two amazing parents already," Rachel told the *New York Post*. "It is crazy because everybody is like, 'She is not your real mom.' And I am like, 'Yeah, she is!'"

Rachel was a sweet, bubbly toddler who fit right in with the Crow clan. She loved playing with her little sister, Hannah, and entertaining her mom and dad with her singing and dancing. She sang her first full song—Faith Hill's "Breathe"—when she was only eighteen months old. And when Rachel was six, she gave her first public performance at a school talent show. It was clear then that Rachel was born to perform. She entered local fairs and contests, but there aren't that many talent scouts in Colorado. So when Rachel was only thirteen years old, her whole family packed up and moved to a tiny two-bedroom house in Los Angeles so Rachel could pursue her dreams of becoming a star.

Chapter 2: X Marks the Spot

Moving to L.A. was a great start, but Rachel still had a long way to go to make her dreams come true. Rachel got her big break when she auditioned to be on a new talent show from the UK called *The X Factor*. Judges for the show included Simon Cowell and Paula Abdul from *American Idol*, music producer L.A. Reid, and pop singer Nicole Scherzinger.

Rachel was one of thousands trying out, but she was the very first audition America got to see when the show aired. She had chosen a difficult song—Duffy's "Mercy"—and she knocked it out of the park. When critiquing her performance, Simon Cowell told the other judges, "Remember these two words: Rachel Crow. Because I think we're going to be hearing a lot about you." Unsurprisingly, all four judges voted her through to the next round!

As the youngest contestant, Rachel was competing against people twice her age! She was often nervous, but she did her best not to let it show. Rachel continued through the audition process, belting out tunes like Whitney Houston's "Run to You" and "I Have Nothing," Beyoncé's "If I Were a Boy," and the Backstreet Boys' "I Want It That Way." Fans loved her.

For the most part, Rachel sailed through the next few rounds, but she did have one close call in the first round after auditions ended.

She sang the Supremes' "Where Did Our Love Go" and Justin Bieber's "Baby." She was one of the low scorers that week, but she was saved by Simon Cowell at the last second. Rachel didn't let her near-miss slow her down, and she went on to dominate for the next four weeks.

Unfortunately for her new fans, Rachel didn't win *The X Factor*. In the sixth week she ended up in the bottom two after singing B.o.B. and Bruno Mars' "Nothin' On You" and Michael Jackson's "Music and Me." The next week she was eliminated after singing Etta James' "I'd Rather Go Blind" for a second time. The judges were very torn, but in the end, Nicole Scherzinger was the deciding vote. Rachel was so shocked that she immediately fell to the floor, sobbing. Eventually, Rachel stopped crying and was able to see that everything was going to be fine. She cheered her new friends on for the rest of the competition and won't miss an episode of the *The X Factor* now. Rachel was

a little embarrassed afterward about getting so upset on TV, as she explained to *Teen Vogue*, "I also overreacted just a little bit, but that was a real reaction. I felt myself wanting to win so badly. I was super sad because I thought everything was over at the time, but it actually had just begun."

Rachel was right: Things were just beginning for her. She just didn't know it then.

Chapter 3: TV Talent

Rachel may not have won *The X Factor*, but she was approached by big-time star-makers Columbia Records, Nickelodeon, and Disney shortly after *The X Factor* ended. After taking several meetings, Rachel signed an overall development deal with Nickelodeon for television and a recording contract with Columbia Records.

Rachel had always wanted to be a singer, but getting the chance to develop her career as an actress, too, was more than she had ever expected. "I am so excited to now be a part of the Nickelodeon family. I grew up watching Nick, and I'm a huge fan," Rachel gushed on rachelcrowofficial.com. Nickelodeon was equally excited to add Rachel to their family. Paula Kaplan, an executive vice president at Nick, really believes in her newest star, as she explained in a press release: "Rachel is an original. She's funny, genuine, and has raw talent and a passion for performing. We're delighted to be home to her first acting project and think she is poised to join the ranks of our next generation of Nick stars."

Rachel couldn't wait to get started, and Nick had plenty planned for her. The network was working hard to write and develop a brand-new comedy and music series for Rachel to star in, but that didn't mean they were going to let her just hang out until it was ready! Rachel dove right into acting.

She competed on Nick's newest game show "Figure It Out" in June 11, 2012. Rachel was a great sport, dancing alongside fellow Nick stars like Lucas Cruikshank and Victoria Justice, and even getting slimed! Gross!

Next up, Rachel guest starred as a superfan on an episode of *Big Time Rush*. She was thrilled to meet the cuties of the boy band, especially since she'd be spending a lot of time with them later when they went on tour together! Kendall, James, Carlos, and Logan treated Rachel just like a sister.

Rachel's biggest guest role so far has been on *Fred: The Show* as a new character named Starr. Starr, like Fred, played by Lucas Cruikshank, is an outsider—but she doesn't let that stop her from going after her dreams. Rachel told *Seventeen* magazine, "My character is fun loving, over-the-top, and very precocious. She's pretty theatrical. . . . I'll be singing so much on *Fred*!"

Rachel loved getting into character as Starr and hanging out with her new co-stars. The whole experience made her really eager to get started on her own show, as she wrote on rachelcrowofficial.com: "I really want it to be something that boys and girls like. I want them to dance and sing and have a ball." With her in the lead role, Rachel's fans are sure to love it!

Chapter 4: Self Titled

Rachel loves acting, but she didn't let her work with Nick get in the way of her first passion—music. Signing with Columbia Records was a huge moment for her, as she wrote on rachelcrowofficial.com: "It's such an honor to be signed to Columbia Records. To think that I am signed to the same label as my idols is a dream come true. I can't wait to get in the studio and start making music."

Completing a full album takes a long time, so Rachel released a self-titled EP, which is a shorter mini-album with just a few songs. *Rachel Crow* gave Rachel's fans their first taste of her original style with five incredible songs. Up until her EP's release, fans had only ever heard Rachel sing covers, but that was about to change! Rachel actually co-wrote her very first single, "Mean Girls," with another writer named Toby Gad. "We sat down and talked about it. He was like, 'How was school for you?' I said, 'I was bullied by the mean girls because I had big, curly hair, this unique personality, and I was different in every way.' We thought it would be a good idea to write a song . . . It's about being yourself and not worrying about what other people think," Rachel told artistdirect.com.

Rachel was very eager to share her personal experiences with her fans, and to help them realize that she really is a regular teen—just like them. "Mean Girls" definitely struck a chord with teen girls, inspiring tweets and Facebook messages from girls who had also been bullied all over the world.

Rachel's other favorite from the EP is "What a Song Can Do," which is all about the importance of music, and how the right song can turn a bad day into a good one. It's the

perfect subject matter for perky Rachel and really sums up how she feels about singing. Rachel's fans love her EP and will be standing in line to buy her full album when it comes out!

Chapter 5: Crowmies

Rachel's fans are very important to her. They are so dedicated that they've even started calling themselves "Crowmies" after Rachel's last name. The Crowmies are always supportive and have cheered for Rachel on some pretty big stages—like at the White House!

Rachel kicked off the annual Easter Egg Roll with the President and First Lady by singing "The Star Spangled Banner" on Easter morning 2012. "The President was amazing . . . you could see that he is just a good person, and he was hilarious. We were talking before we went out, and he was telling us all how he was going to beat a three year old at the Easter Egg Roll. It was amazing," Rachel told blog.scholastic.com. It was an especially sweet moment for Rachel since President Obama has been one of her heroes for a long time.

Rachel went on her very first tour during the summer of 2012 as part of Big Time Rush's "Big Time Summer Tour" along with fellow pop star Cody Simpson. Rachel already knew all of the guys, so that helped make the tour even more fun.

Rachel got to perform all of her songs from her EP on the tour—plus a few fun covers. Her set included a giant boom box, blow-up flowers, and plenty of flashing lights. Rachel loves performing, but she still gets nervous sometimes. "I always make sure to run through the song in my head once just to make sure I got it. I usually don't get nervous the whole day if I know I'm performing, but literally right before I go on, I'm like, 'Oh no, oh no, oh okay, yay! I'm out on stage, I'm happier.' Usually when I'm right behind the scenes, one minute before the show, I get a little bit nervous. But I think everybody does," Rachel confessed to *Twist*.

Despite pre-show jitters, Rachel was a hit with all of the Crowmies that showed up to cheer her on. They'll definitely be buying tickets for her future shows and are hoping Rachel will be headlining her own tour soon!

Chapter 6: Behind the Scenes

The life of a pop star isn't all fun concerts and TV shows. Rachel spends a lot of time going to events, giving interviews, or doing photo shoots. She always works very hard, but that doesn't mean things go perfectly every time, as she confessed to blog.scholastic.com. "I recently had a photo shoot, and they decided they wanted a candle on the desk. So, I'm taking my tutu off, and I put it over the candle and a fire starts, and all you hear is *'Beep!*

Beep!' and me going, 'Heeeelp!' in the other room. And so the stylist walks in. She goes, 'Oh my gosh,' and my mom, she can't even move—she's freaking out—and I'm ducked behind the table, like, freaking out. They put out the fire. It was terrible. It was a 'Rachel moment' times a million. Everything was fine but the tutu."

When Rachel isn't working, she tries to spend as much time as possible hanging out with her friends and family. Rachel gets advice from her mom and dad on just about everything, and she's super-close with her sister. They love going swimming, watching movies, and just goofing off together.

Shopping and getting her hair and nails done are some of Rachel's favorite things to do! She has a bright, fun fashion sense. Rachel loves brightly colored skinny jeans, tutus and other full skirts, printed blazers, sequins, and Converse high-tops. She's also well known for her super-curly hair, which she wears in a natural Afro or fun up-dos. And she never forgets her nails—one of her playful manicures was even featured on the popular blog hellogiggles.com!

Rachel works hard to give back whenever she can. She is dedicated to speaking out against bullying and has been working with dosomething.org's "The Bully Project" to help educate teens about the damage that bullying can do and to provide support for teens facing bullying. Rachel also really wants to start a foundation for fellow foster kids. She knows what it's like to be in that situation, and she wants to help other foster kids find permanent homes while supporting them as they work to achieve their dreams, too.

Chapter 7: What's Next?

So, what's on the horizon for this bubbly popstar and actress? Plenty! Between filming her new show for Nickelodeon and working on her first full-length album,

Rachel is staying very busy. She's working with different songwriters, producers, and collaborators to perfect her sound, and it's very important to Rachel that she get it right. "I want my first album to have a lot of high notes in songs. I want there to be upbeat songs and slow songs, I want it to be retro and very soulful, and I want at least one of my songs to have a guy rapping in it, because that is just so cool," Rachel told MTV.com.

Rachel has been equally thoughtful about her show for Nickelodeon. It's really important to her that her show will make people laugh and allow for some awesome musical performances. Rachel is just starting to achieve her dreams, and, since she's only a teenager, she has plenty of time ahead of her. She'd love to star in movies, release multiple albums, and headline her own tour someday. But for now, Rachel is just taking things one day at a time and enjoying every minute of it!

Just the Facts

Name: Rachel Crow

Birthday: January 23, 1998

Hometown: Mead, Colorado

Parents: Barbara and Kelly Crow

Siblings: younger sister, Hannah

Hair: dark brown and curly

Eyes: brown

Pet: a Maltese-Yorkie puppy named Charlie

Favorite Movie: *Titanic*

Favorite Flowers: daisies

Favorite Color: sky blue

Favorite Foods: Chinese food and chocolate

Favorite Books: Diary of a Wimpy Kid series and The Dork Diaries serie

Hobbies: Doodling, swimming, and going to the movies

Favorite Singers: Eminem, Beyoncé, Adele, Bruno Mars

Official Website:
www.rachelcrowofficial.com
Official Twitter: iamrachelcrow
Official Facebook: iamrachelcrow
Official instagram: iamrachelcrow